Love to Quilt...

BEARS
BEARS
BEARS

Love to Quilt...

BEARS
BEARS
BEARS

Karen Kay Buckley

American Quilter's Society

P. O. Box 3290 • Paducah, KY 42002-3290

Located in Paducah, Kentucky, the American Quilter's Society (AQS), is dedicated to promoting the accomplishments of today's quilters. Through its publications and events, AQS strives to honor today's quiltmakers and their work – and inspire future creativity and innovation in quiltmaking.

Book Design – Elaine Wilson
Illustrations – Whitney Hopkins and Elaine Wilson
Cover Design – Elaine Wilson
Photography – Charles R. Lynch

Library of Congress Cataloging-in-Publication Data

Buckley, Karen Kay.
    Love to quilt--bears, bears, bears / Karen Kay Buckley.
        p.   cm.
    ISBN 0-89145-881-6
    1. Patchwork--Patterns. 2. Appliqué--Patterns. 3. Children's quilts. 4. Soft toy making. 5. Teddy bears in art. I. Title.
    TT835.B7824 1996
    746.46'041--dc21   96-37102
                                         CIP

Additional copies of this book may be ordered from: American Quilter's Society, P.O. Box 3290, Paducah, KY 42002-3290 @ $14.95. Add $2.00 for postage & handling.

bearsbearsbearsbearsbearsbearsbearsbearsbearsbearsbearsbearsbearsbearsbearsbearsbearsbearsbearsbearsbearsbearsbearsbearsbearsbearsbears

Bears, Bears, Bears

Acknowledgments

The most important person in my life is my husband, Joe. Without his support and encouragement I would never have completed this book. Thanks Joe. You are my best friend, and I am looking forward to many more great adventures together.

I need to especially thank two people for their work on the plaid bear quilt: Kathy Eberwein did such a great job putting the top together, and Sandy Chambers did an excellent job quilting. They both worked under a short deadline, and it was well worth their efforts. I always wondered how this quilt would look in plaids and now I know!

A very special thanks to Linda Rudy-Price who also worked under a great deal of pressure. When this book was close to completion, I suggested including a stuffed bear pattern. I had worked with Linda years ago selling her wonderful teddy bears when I owned my quilt shop. I asked her to design a new bear for the book. She was kind enough to say yes, and it is a great addition to the book.

Thanks also to Meredith Schroeder who was always there when I had questions and supports all quilters.

Bears, Bears, Bears

Contents

BEARS, BEARS, BEARS, 39½" x 60½", 1996, Kathy Eberwein, quilted by Sandy Chambers. Stuffed bears by Linda Rudy-Price.

Introduction

The idea for this quilt pattern came about when my sister, Paula, was pregnant. I wanted to make a special quilt for her second child, Laurel. Paula had decided on teddy bear wallpaper for the new baby's room. That got me started.

Years ago I was told that I needed to find my niche, either to piece or to appliqué. Well, I find that my niche combines both! The quilts you see in this book combine hand appliqué with machine piecing. However, you could piece by hand and do machine appliqué if that is your niche. This book will not go into a lot of detail about appliqué and will assume you have a favorite technique. If you need some help, my first book, *From Basics to Binding: A Complete Guide to Making Quilts* (hand appliqué) and my second book *Above and Beyond Basics* (both hand and machine appliqué) go into great detail on the many techniques to achieve good points and nice, smooth curves.

Basic Information to Get Started

Fabric

I recommend working with pre-washed 100% cotton fabric. It is soft and makes most of the appliqué techniques much easier to accomplish. Make sure the fabric is colorfast before starting the project. (This is the voice of experience, unfortunately!)

When selecting colors for the quilt, consider a theme fabric. The fabrics for the plaid quilt were selected based on the multicolored border fabric. If a multicolored fabric catches your eye, carry the bolt around the quilt shop with you and match other fabrics to it. It is an easy way to start and you can add other colors as you feel the need. The idea of a theme fabric always produces a great looking quilt. The pastel quilt colors were selected by taking a piece of the wallpaper to the quilt shop and matching the colors. It sure looks great hanging in Laurel's room, along with all her stuffed teddy bears.

Sewing Machine

Make sure your machine is in good working condition. Clean your machine after every ten hours of sewing. Depending on how much sewing you do, take your machine into the dealer to have it cleaned and serviced once or twice a year. The service person can get to areas on the machine that you cannot. If your machine operates well, it makes your sewing experience much better. Along with the cleaning,

do not forget to oil your machine. Your owner's manual will tell you where and how often this needs to be done.

You should change the needle on your sewing machine after about ten hours of sewing. If you hear a popping noise while sewing, that means the point of the needle is dull and needs to be changed. A dull needle can cause damage to the fabric, so remember to change that needle regularly.

Thread

For machine piecing, consider using 100% cotton 50/3 thread. It works great in the machine and if you are using cotton fabric, cotton thread is recommended.

For hand appliqué I strongly encourage you to use 100% cotton 60/2 thread. It is thinner than regular sewing weight thread and makes your appliqué work look better. The thread is so fine that it gets lost on the appliqué and all you see is the nice smooth edges. Because this thread is so thin it does not have to perfectly match the appliqué fabric. Match it as closely as you can. If you are having trouble finding a matching thread, try a shade of gray. Gray seems to work well with many colors.

Pins

For appliqué and piecing I prefer silk pins. They are thinner, go in and out of the fabric better, and do not distort the seams. The thickness of the pins does make a difference. Some thicker pins can cause the lower fabric to be pushed out of line which can result in poor points on your pieced seams. To make those points line up nicely, read the section on Matching Seams.

Bias Press Bars

These are used to make stems, basket handles, Celtic designs, and the jump rope on one of the appliqué bears in this book.

Pressing

For the pieced blocks use a dry, hot iron. Early in my quilting career I worked with steam and found that it distorted and stretched the seams. Press the pieced seams on the back to one side. Then press the seam again on the top. If there are any tucks or puckers in the seam, you will have problems assembling the quilt top; they will alter its size. The time it takes to press those seams is well worth the results.

The only time I use steam is to press the large pieces of fabric after they are washed. Using steam at this stage helps to remove the wrinkles.

Cutting Tools and Suggestions

The instructions in this book are to cut the fabric for the pieced blocks using a rotary cutter. You will need a rotary cutter, board, and ruler. If you have not worked with a rotary cutter before, please check at your local quilt shop for a book on techniques and methods. There are several good ones available.

One suggestion for cutting the triangle shapes for the pieced blocks is to layer your fabric. For example, if you are working with a white background and a blue fabric, place these two fabrics right sides together. Fol-

low the directions for cutting. These two triangles will be sewn together to make the Bear's Paw block. If they are cut together, you will not have to spend time lining up the edges. This little trick not only saves time but allows greater accuracy. (This would also apply to the two larger triangles in the Bear's Paw block.)

Sewing Suggestions and Matching Seams

When trying to get the points on the pieced blocks to line up, using the center pin idea works very well. Place the two points you need to meet right sides together. Place one pin through the X, but do not secure the pin. This pin I use for positioning only. Place a pin on each side of the point through the top and bottom layers of fabric. Remove the center positioning pin. When machine piecing you sew from raw edge to raw edge of the fabric. An X will be created at the seam area. Sew through the X in the thread and you will have a perfect point every time (Fig. 1). Well, almost every time!

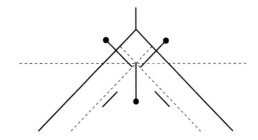

Fig. 1.

Most sewers are consistent in sewing a ¼" seam allowance and pressing seams. So pieced blocks will all come out to be the same size, or very close. My recommendation is to make the pieced blocks first and measure the blocks. They should be 11" x 11" from raw edge to raw edge. However, if yours are slightly different, you can cut the background squares accordingly. If you cut the background squares for the appliqué first and find your Bear's Paw blocks came out slightly larger, it will be difficult to piece the top together. (Maybe this is why I like combining piecing and appliqué. You can make the top fit together!)

Faces on the Appliqué Bears

The faces on the appliqué bears were drawn by using Pigma® permanent markers. The Pigma® markers do not bleed onto the fabric and allow you to draw accurate lines. My husband, Joe, drew the faces on the two bear quilts I made. I am always afraid to use the permanent marker after I have done all that hand appliqué; but Joe has no fear and always does a wonderful job. This allows Joe to be part of the gift-giving experience!

You could work at a light box or a window during the day. Tape the pattern to the glass. Place the fabric over the pattern and trace the eyes, mouth, and nose. On the plaid quilt made by Kathy Eberwein, the fabric for the bears was darker. The marker would never have been seen. Instead of marking pencils, Kathy used some very small buttons for the eyes. They worked great. It may depend on how the quilt will be used whether you use buttons or not. If you think the quilt will be used in a crib and not just hung as a display, consider using embroidery stitches or Pigma® markers on the eyes. If you like to do embroidery, the entire face could be done with embroidery stitching. Please make sure the thread is colorfast before using it in your quilt.

Stuffed Teddy Bears

Supplies

Paper scissors

Fabric scissors

Thread to match fabric

Sewing machine in good working order

Sewing needle

Quilting thread to match main fabric

Ribbon to place around neck of bear

Tissue paper to trace pattern

Arm and leg joints

Safety eyes and nose

Fiberfil® to stuff the bear

Skein of black embroidery floss

Large Bear

¾ yard main fabric

¼ yard for muzzle, inside ears, feet, and
hands (complimentary color)

4 – 55mm joints

2 – 12mm safety eyes

1 – 18mm safety nose

2 – 16 oz. bags of poly Fiberfil®

Scraps of batting

1 skein of black embroidery floss

1 yard of ribbon for around neck

Small Bear

½ yard main fabric

⅛ yard for muzzle, inside ears, feet, and
hands (complimentary color)

4 – 30mm joints

2 – 9mm safety eyes

1 – 15mm safety nose

1 – 16 oz. bag of poly Fiberfil®

Scraps of batting

1 skein of black embroidery floss

1 yard of ribbon for around neck

Cutting Instructions

From your smaller complimentary piece of
fabric cut the following:

- Cut 2 A pieces – ears
- Cut 2 B pieces – paws
- Cut 2 C pieces – footpads
- Cut 2 D pieces – muzzle

From your batting cut the following:

- Cut 2 A pieces – ears

From your main fabric cut the following:

- Cut 2 A pieces – ears
- Cut 2 E pieces – sides of head
- Cut 1 F piece – center of head
- Cut 2 G pieces – front belly pieces
- Cut 2 H pieces – outside of arms
- Cut 2 J pieces – inside of each arm
- Cut 4 K pieces – legs
- Cut 2 L pieces – back of body

General Instructions

Sew all seams with a ¼" seam allowance. Pattern pieces include the ¼" seam allowance.

The arrow on each pattern piece indicates the direction of the grain.

The double slash marks on the pattern pieces indicate the sides that do not get sewn. These areas need to be left unsewn in order to turn the piece inside out.

When turning pieces inside out, clip the curves to give a smoother seam.

Most of the seams do not need to be pressed after they are sewn because the stuffing will push the seams open. If pressing is recommended, it is noted.

Backstitching is recommended where you start and where you finish at every seam and dart.

Tracing and Transferring the Pattern

Place the tissue paper over the pattern pieces and trace, including any markings or notations. With your paper scissors, cut on the lines you just drew. Do not add a seam allowance. It has already been included in the pattern. Pin the pattern pieces to the fabric. (If you layer your fabric in two before pinning, it will save a lot of cutting time.) Cut around the edges of each pattern piece.

Sewing Instructions

- Place an A piece from the main fabric and an A piece from the complimentary fabric right sides together. Lay a batting ear on the back side of the main fabric. Sew around the curved sides. Remember, do not sew on those sides marked with the double slash marks. Turn the pieces inside out. Push the seams open with your fingers to smooth the curves. Top-stitch ¼" from the folded edge.

- Sew the darts in pieces E and F. In order to sew the darts, fold the fabric right sides together along the dart lines. Sew on the dotted lines. For a smooth dart, try to sew from the outside edge to the point of the dart.

- After sewing them, place the ears along the right side of the E piece and pin in place. Fold the other side of the E piece marked "ear" on top of this seam and sew from the point out to the outside edge. About 1¼" of the ear will be hanging out of the seam. Do not worry! This will be caught in the next seam.

- Pin piece E and piece F right sides together. Be sure the section of the ear that extended beyond the seam on the previous section is folded so the ear will come to the front of the bear. Repeat for other side.

- With right sides together, pin piece D to the section you have just sewn. Be sure to match the notches. You will need to ease this seam. After this seam is sewn, clip the seam allowance so it will lay flatter when it is opened.

- Sew the bottom of the muzzle and the neck seam. Turn head right side out.

- Sew the G pieces together by placing them right sides together. Sew along the center front seam.

- Sew the L pieces together down the back seam.

- Now join the front to the back along the side seams of G and L.

- Sew piece B to piece J by matching the notches. Press the seam. Place these sections right sides together with piece H and sew. Be sure to leave open the area marked "leave open" in order to turn the arms inside out. Repeat for the other arm. Turn the arms inside out through the opening.

- Place K pieces right sides together. Sew around the edges, but be sure to leave the area marked "leave open" unsewn in order to turn the legs inside out. Do not sew the edge marked with the double slash marks. Pin piece C in place. Sew the footpad seam. Turn the legs inside out through the opening along the side.

Assembling the Joints of the Arms and Legs

To assemble the joints for the arms and legs, cut small slits where the joints are marked on the pattern pieces. These slits should only be about ¼". Cut some scraps of batting the same size as the joint. You need to cut 16 of these in all. Place 2 pieces of batting on the stem of the joint. Insert inside arms and/or legs. Push through corresponding slit in body area. (Be sure to insert on the inside of the arm and not the outside. This is the voice of experience.) After the stem is on the inside of the arm and/or leg, place 2 pieces of batting over the stem. Now place the washer on the stem and then the snap piece. You will hear a clicking noise. Push as far as it will go. You need to push hard to get a good tight joint.

Stuffing the Body, Arms, and Legs

To stuff the bear use small amounts of Fiberfil® and push it into each area gradually. Use your fingers to push into the small areas until stuffing is firm. The handle of a wooden spoon can be helpful when stuffing smaller areas. Sew openings closed using an appliqué or ladder stitch.

Eyes, Nose, and Stuffing the Head

Insert eyes and nose. Again, this will be similar to the joint pieces. Place a very small slit where you plan to place the eye/nose piece. Place small pieces of batting on the stem of the eye/nose and push through the slit. Once the stem is on the inside, place the rubber washer on the stem. You will hear a clicking noise just like when you did the arm and leg joints. After the eyes and nose have been attached you are ready to stuff the head.

Attaching the Head to the Body

Using quilting thread and a large needle sew the head to the body by hand. Sew around the neck area three times to make sure it is secure and sturdy. Sewing the head a little off center can give the bear some personality! Experiment tilting the head before sewing.

Mouth Area

Using three strands of embroidery floss, sew a smile on the muzzle of your bear. Again, experiment with a small or large smile.

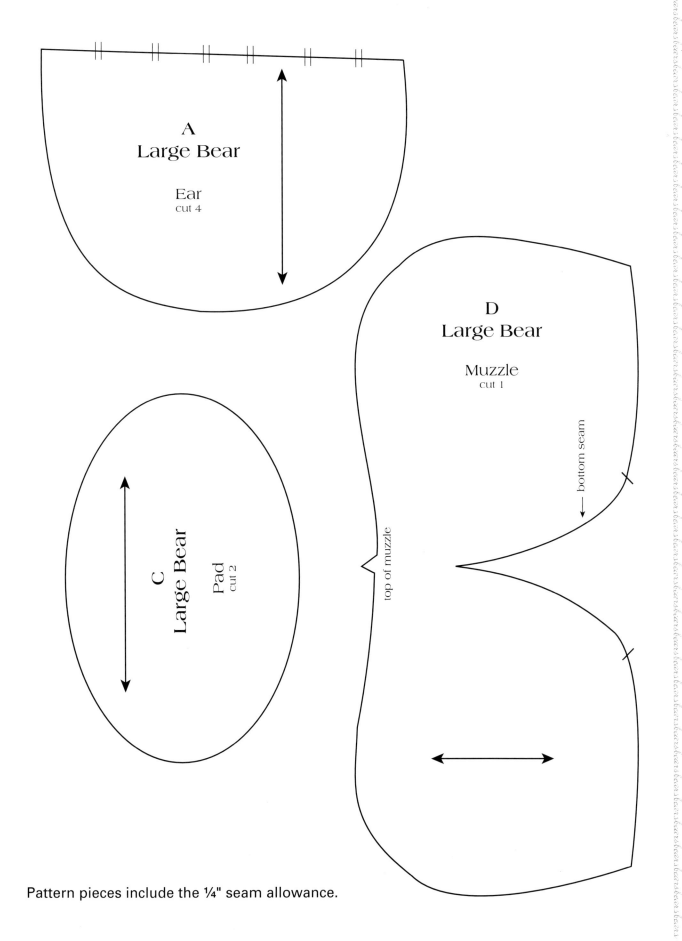

A
Large Bear

Ear
cut 4

D
Large Bear

Muzzle
cut 1

← bottom seam

top of muzzle

C
Large Bear

Pad
cut 2

Pattern pieces include the ¼" seam allowance.

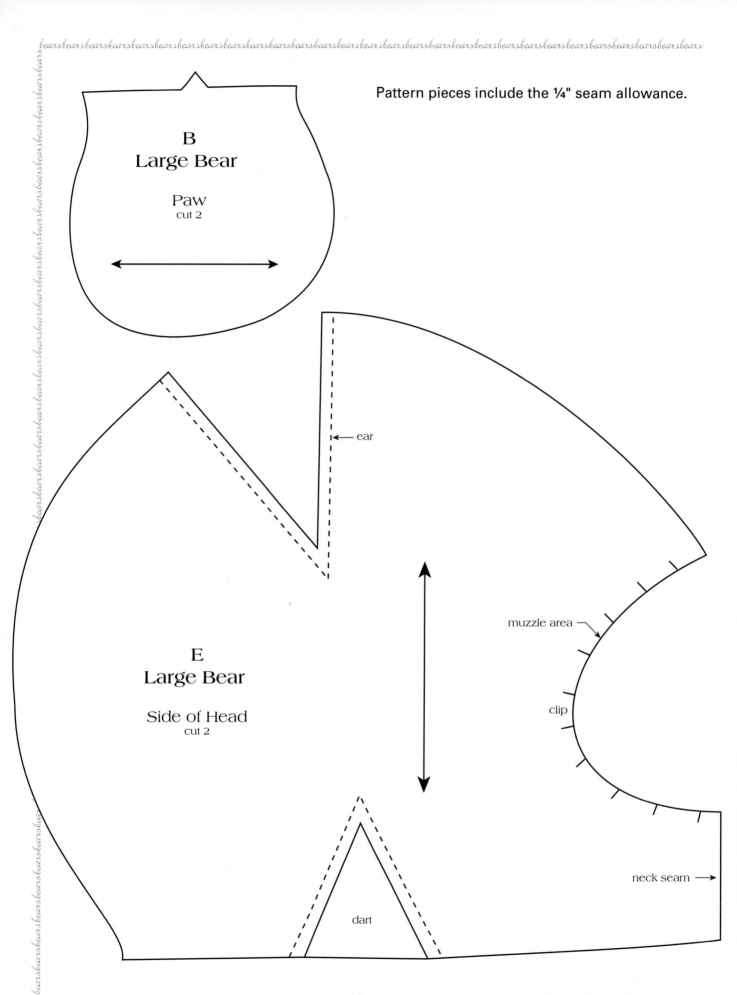

Pattern pieces include the ¼" seam allowance.

B
Large Bear

Paw
cut 2

ear

muzzle area

clip

E
Large Bear

Side of Head
cut 2

neck seam

dart

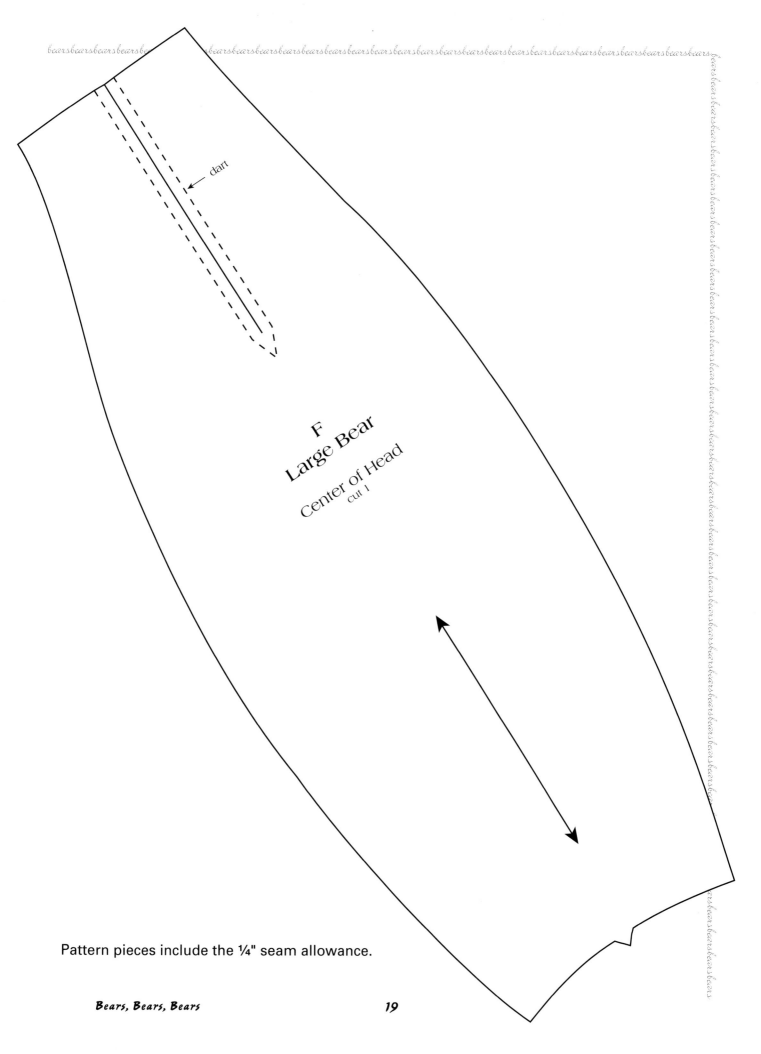

dart

F
Large Bear
Center of Head
cut 1

Pattern pieces include the ¼" seam allowance.

BEARS, BEARS, BEARS, 39½" x 60½", Karen Kay Buckley.

Bear by Linda Rudy-Price. Quilt by Kathy Eberwein, quilted by Sandy Chambers.

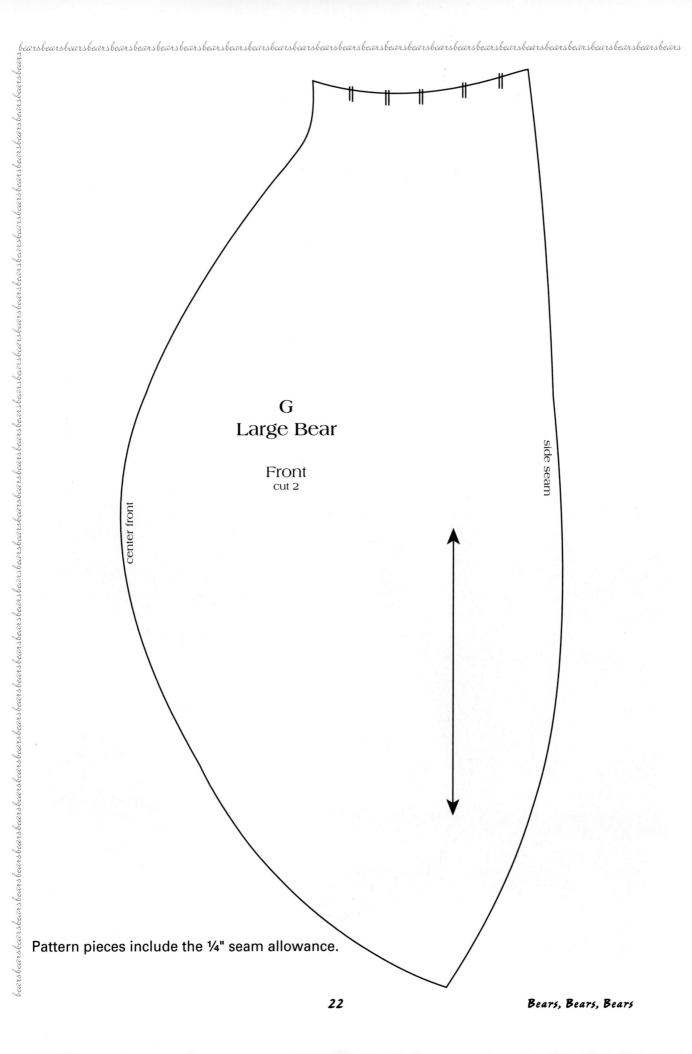

G
Large Bear

Front
cut 2

center front

side seam

Pattern pieces include the ¼" seam allowance.

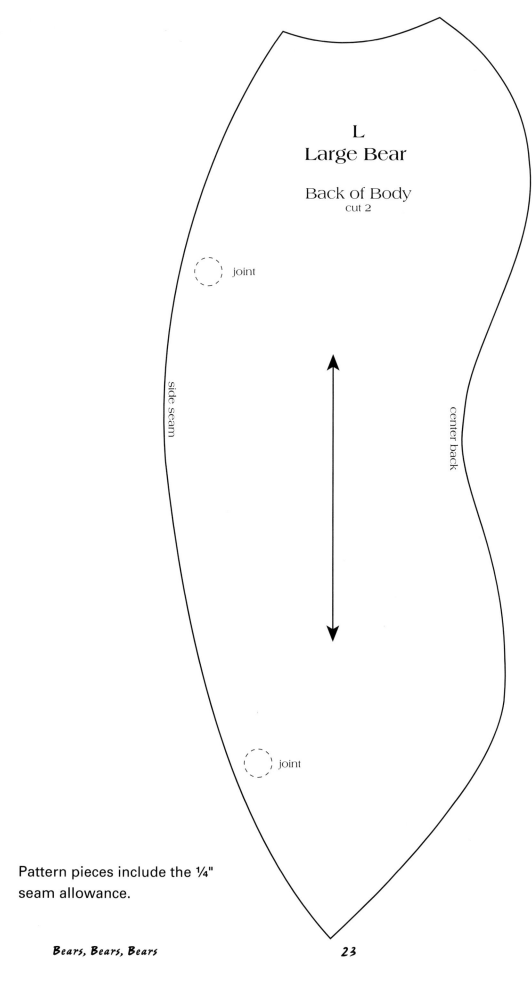

L
Large Bear

Back of Body
cut 2

joint

side seam

center back

joint

Pattern pieces include the ¼"
seam allowance.

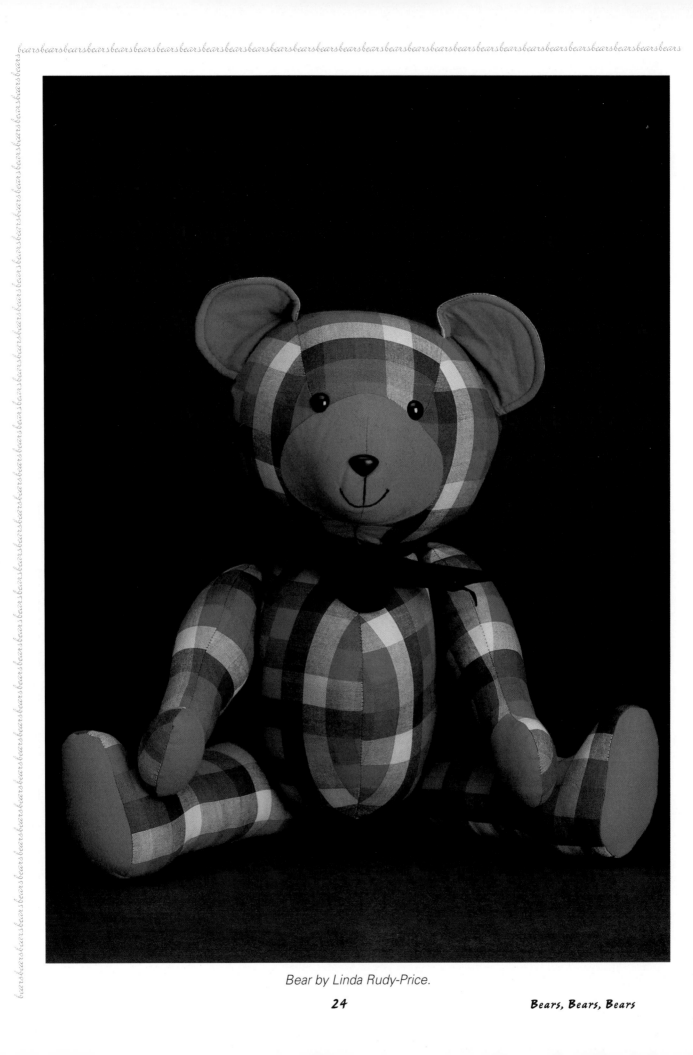

Bear by Linda Rudy-Price.

BEARS, BEARS, BEARS, 39½" x 60½," 1996,
Kathy Eberwein, quilted by Sandy Chambers.

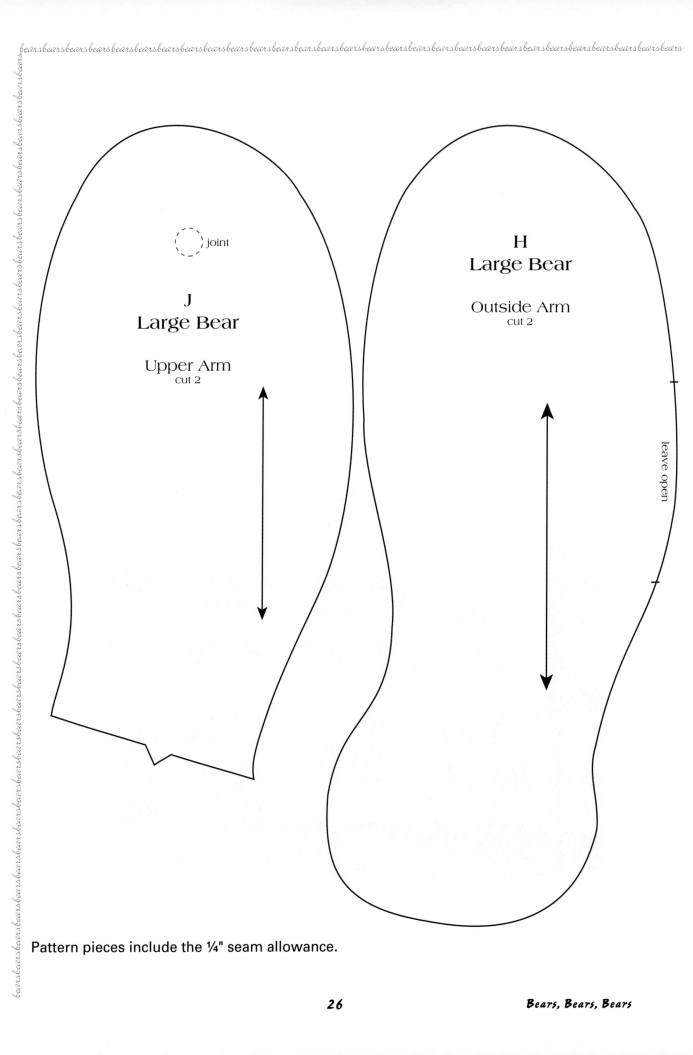

joint

J
Large Bear

Upper Arm
cut 2

H
Large Bear

Outside Arm
cut 2

leave open

Pattern pieces include the ¼" seam allowance.

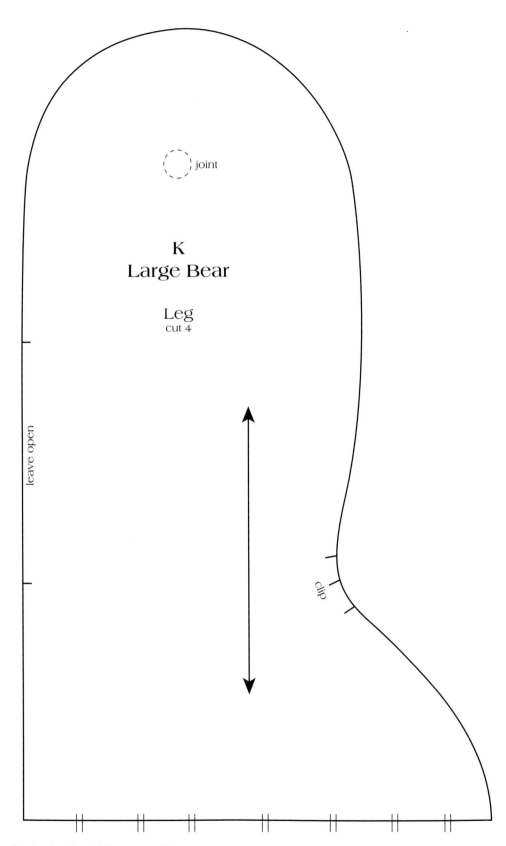

K
Large Bear

Leg
cut 4

joint

leave open

clip

Pattern pieces include the ¼" seam allowance.

Bear by Linda Rudy-Price. Quilt by Kathy Eberwein, quilted by Sandy Chambers.

Bear by Linda Rudy-Price.

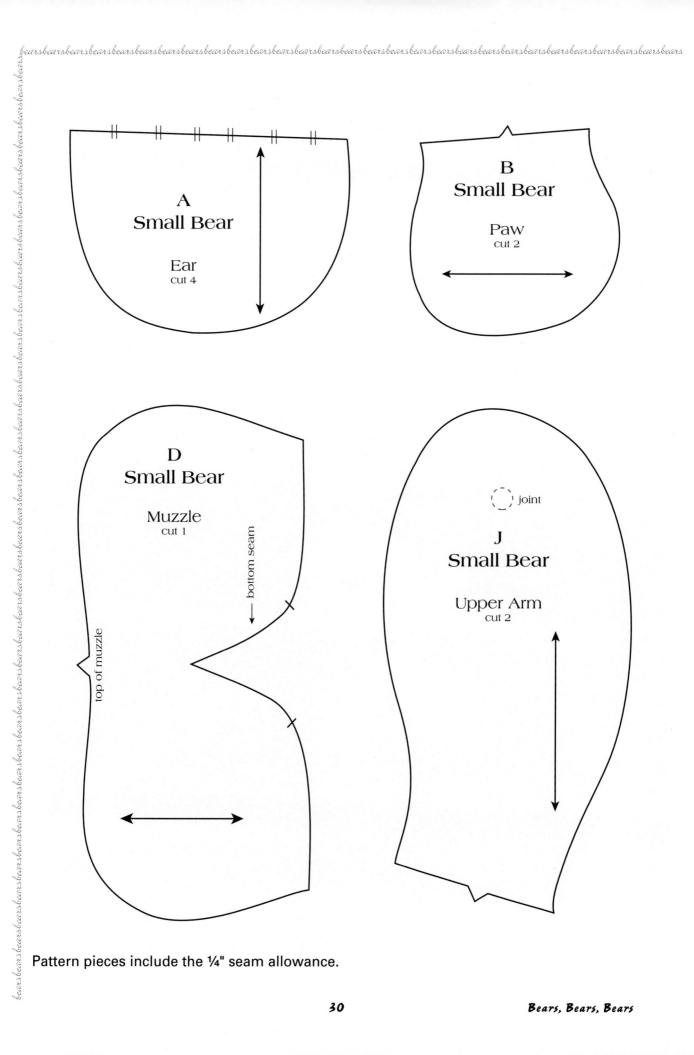

Pattern pieces include the ¼" seam allowance.

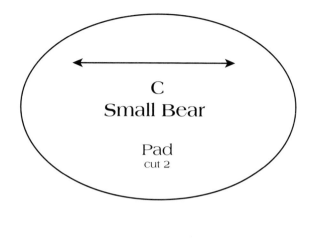

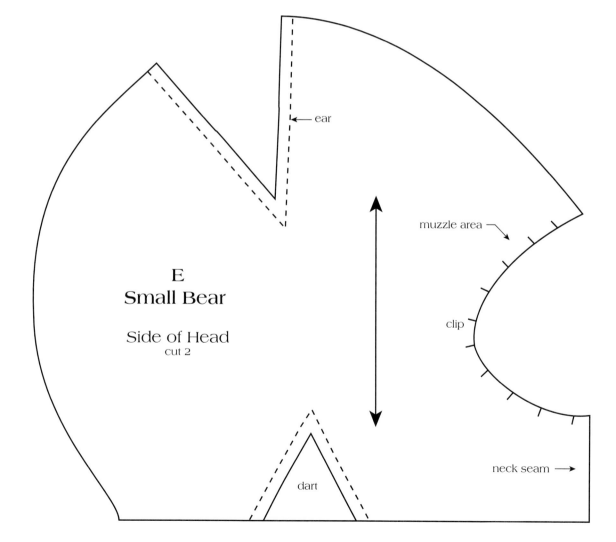

Pattern pieces include the ¼" seam allowance.

BEARS, BEARS, BEARS, 60½" x 39½", Karen Kay Buckley.

Bears, Bears, Bears

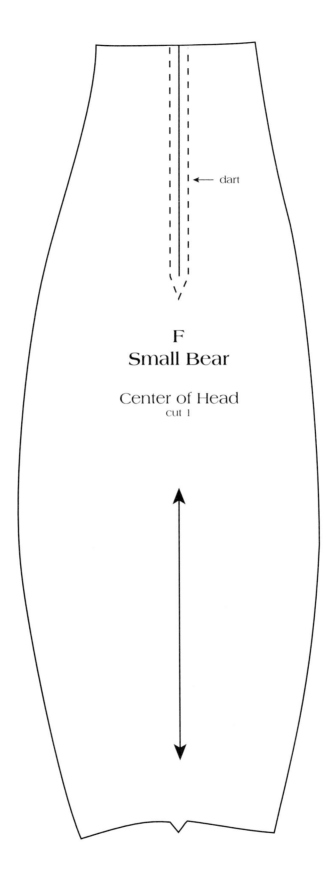

← dart

F
Small Bear

Center of Head
cut 1

Pattern pieces include the ¼" seam allowance.

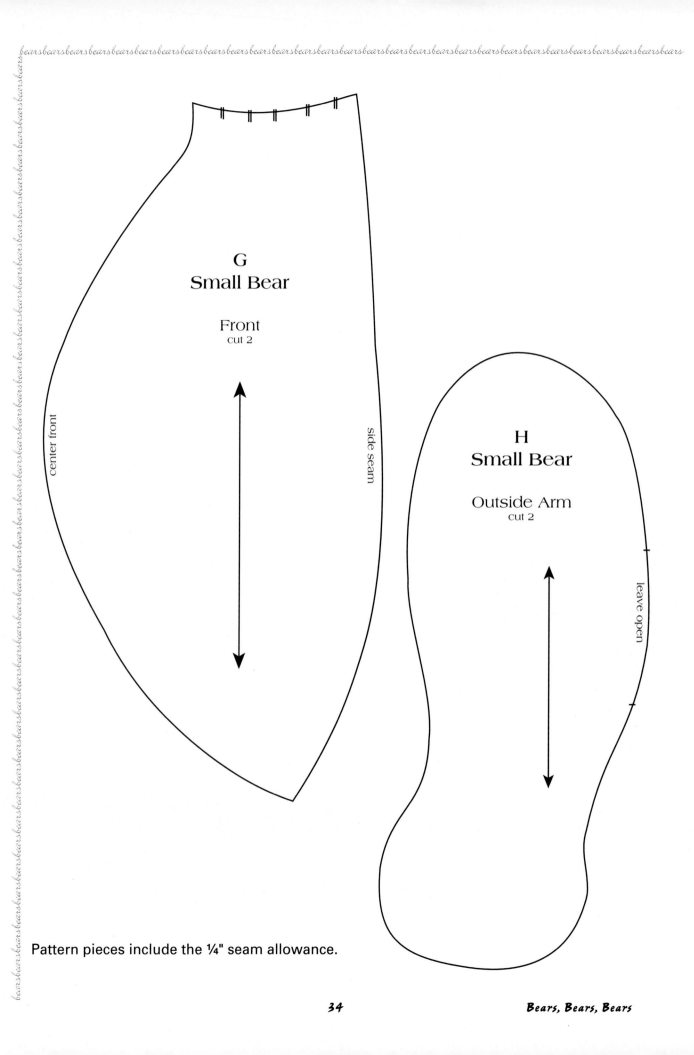

G
Small Bear

Front
cut 2

center front

side seam

H
Small Bear

Outside Arm
cut 2

leave open

Pattern pieces include the ¼" seam allowance.

Pattern pieces include the ¼" seam allowance.

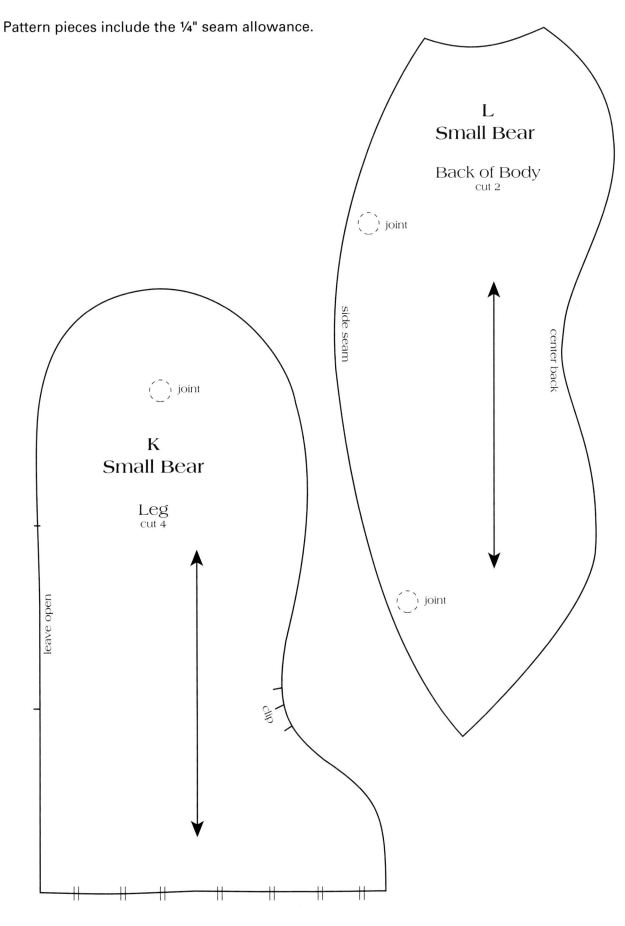

L
Small Bear

Back of Body
cut 2

joint

side seam

center back

joint

joint

K
Small Bear

Leg
cut 4

leave open

clip

Bears, Bears, Bears

I just love this project. My husband and I designed the bears and Joe transferred all of their faces to the fabric. This is a great project for a baby quilt and for those people who love and collect bears. The purple, pink, and blue one was made for my niece, Laurel. It matches the bear wallpaper in her room. Hand or machine appliqué can be used for the bears.

The finished size of this piece is 39½" x 60½".

Supplies

Rotary cutter

Cutting board

Ruler

Thread to match for piecing and appliqué

Sewing machine

Fabric scissors

Paper scissors

Silk pins

Permanent Pigma marker, or embroidery thread for the faces

Bias Press Bar® for jumping rope bear

Supplies necessary for the appliqué method of your choice

Fabric

> **Bold letters are for the primary colored quilt, p. 20.**
> *Italicized letters are for the pastel colored quilt, p. 32.*
> **Script letters are for the plaid quilt, p. 25.**

3 yards for the background (includes border) (applies to primary and pastel quilts)

¾ yard **blue** (*light blue*) **(blue)**, includes piecing, appliqué, and binding

⅝ yard **green** (*purple*) **(green)**, includes piecing, appliqué, and binding

⅝ yard **red** (*dark blue*) **(pink)**, includes piecing, appliqué, and binding

¼ yard **yellow** (*pink*) **(yellow)**, includes piecing and appliqué

⅜ yard dark brown for bears

⅛ yard light brown or scraps for the muzzles on the bears

Special instructions for the plaid quilt:

2 yards plaid for border

½ yard for binding. Both the primary and pastel bindings were made by cutting strips from the scraps left over after the appliqué.

The plaid quilt used two different background fabrics:

¾ yard background behind appliqué

⅞ yard background for pieced blocks

Cutting Instructions

From the background fabric:

- Cut two border strips 45" x 4½" and two strips, along the selvage, 66" x 4½".
- Cut 32 – 2" x 5" rectangles.
- Cut 32 – 2" squares.
- Cut 64 – 2⅜" squares, cut into half-square triangles (Fig. 2). You will need 128 of these triangles.
- Cut 7 – 11" squares for the appliqué.

From the **blue** *(light blue)* **(blue)**:

- Cut 64 – 2⅜" squares. Cut these into half-square triangles (Fig. 2).

From the **green** *(purple)* **(green)**:

- Cut 16 – 3⅞" squares. Cut these into half-square triangles (Fig. 2).

From the **red** *(dark blue)* **(pink)**:

- Cut 16 – 3⅞" squares. Cut these into half-square triangles (Fig. 2).

From the **yellow** *(pink)* **(yellow)**:

- Cut 8 – 2" squares.

Sewing Instructions for Pieced Blocks

- Sew one **blue** *(light blue)* **(blue)** triangle to one background triangle (Fig. 3). You will need 128 of these units. Press the seams toward the **blue** *(lighter blue)* **(blue)** fabric.
- Sew a center **yellow** *(pink)* **(yellow)** square between two 2" x 5" background pieces (Fig. 4). Press the seams toward the background fabric, unless there is a problem with the fabric shadowing. (On the white quilt it was necessary to press the seams toward the yellow fabric because the

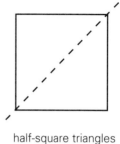

Fig. 2. Cutting half-square triangles.

Fig. 3. Sew one 2⅜" dark triangle to one 2⅜" light triangle.

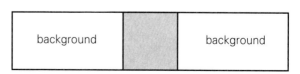

Fig. 4. Center square between two background pieces. Press toward the darker fabric.

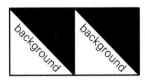

Fig. 5. Sew two units together.

Fig. 6. Sew a 2" square to the previous unit.

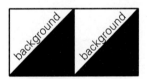

Fig. 7. Sew two units together.

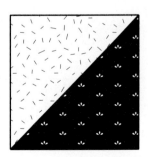

Fig. 8. Sew two 3⅛" triangles together.

yellow shadowed through the white.)

- Sew 32 **blue** *(light blue)* **(blue)** and background units into sections that look like Fig. 5. Be sure they are exactly in this direction. Press so you can see the outer points.
- Sew a background square to each of the previous units and press toward the background, unless you have a shadowing problem (Fig. 6).
- Sew 32 **blue** *(light blue)* **(blue)** units into sections that look like Figure 7. Again, be sure they are exactly in this direction and press so you can see the outer points.
- Sew 28 **red** *(dark blue)* **(pink)** and **green** *(purple)* **(green)** units together. Press these seams toward the **red** *(dark blue)* **(pink)** (Fig. 8).
- Pin and sew a **blue** *(light blue)* **(blue)** and background section to each side of a **red** *(dark blue)* **(pink)** and **green** *(purple)* **(green)** section. Be sure they are all in the correct direction (Fig. 9). (You want the marked points to meet, so pin them in place. It will make the later steps much easier.)
- Complete the paw section by sewing the previous sections together (Fig. 10).
- Sew the block together as in Fig. 11. Row one and three are made from the pieced sections, plus a 2" x 5" background piece. Press the seams toward the rectangular shapes.
- You need eight of these Bear Paw blocks.

Appliqué

Transfer the appliqué patterns onto the background fabric. The lines down the center of each design are the centering lines.

Some tips on the appliqué, quilting, and binding.

- *The appliqué pieces are lettered in the order of placement.* There is no letter "I."
- On the "bear with the baby blocks" (page 41), piece the blocks and then appliqué them.
- On the "bear standing on its head" block (page 42), sew six 1" x 3" strips together to make the shirt.
- On the "bear with the ball" block (page 43), sew the ball shape together by sewing the curved seams. Then sew the ball shape to the background fabric.
- On the "bear with the honey pot" block (page 44), cut the shirt as one big piece and then appliqué the stripe to the shirt.
- On the "bear with the jump rope" block (page 45), cut the rope 1" on the bias, and use the ³⁄₁₆" Bias Press Bar®.
- Quilt as shown in Fig. 12, page 40. Continue the lines from the blocks straight out into the border. The lines follow the seams on the pieced Bear's Paw blocks. Quilt in the ditch around the appliqué shapes.
- On the primary colored quilt, rainbow binding was used. Sew 2" wide strips together until the length is 230".
- On the pastel quilt, only purple and blue fabrics were alternated to make the binding.

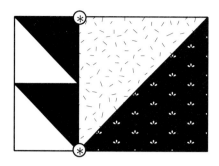

Fig. 9. Pin blue backgrounds to red/pink/green sections.

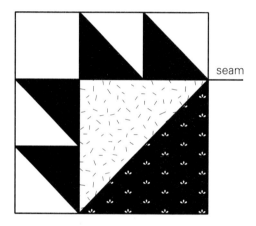

Fig. 10. Complete the block.

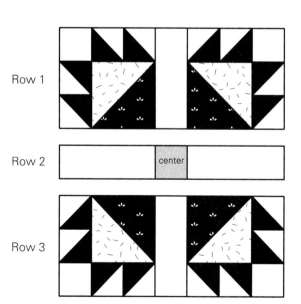

Fig. 11. Assemble the blocks.

Bears, Bears, Bears   *39*

Fig. 12. Quilting diagram.

Bears, Bears, Bears

center

bears

center

A

B

J

K

E

G

H

F

C

D

L

Bears, Bears, Bears

43

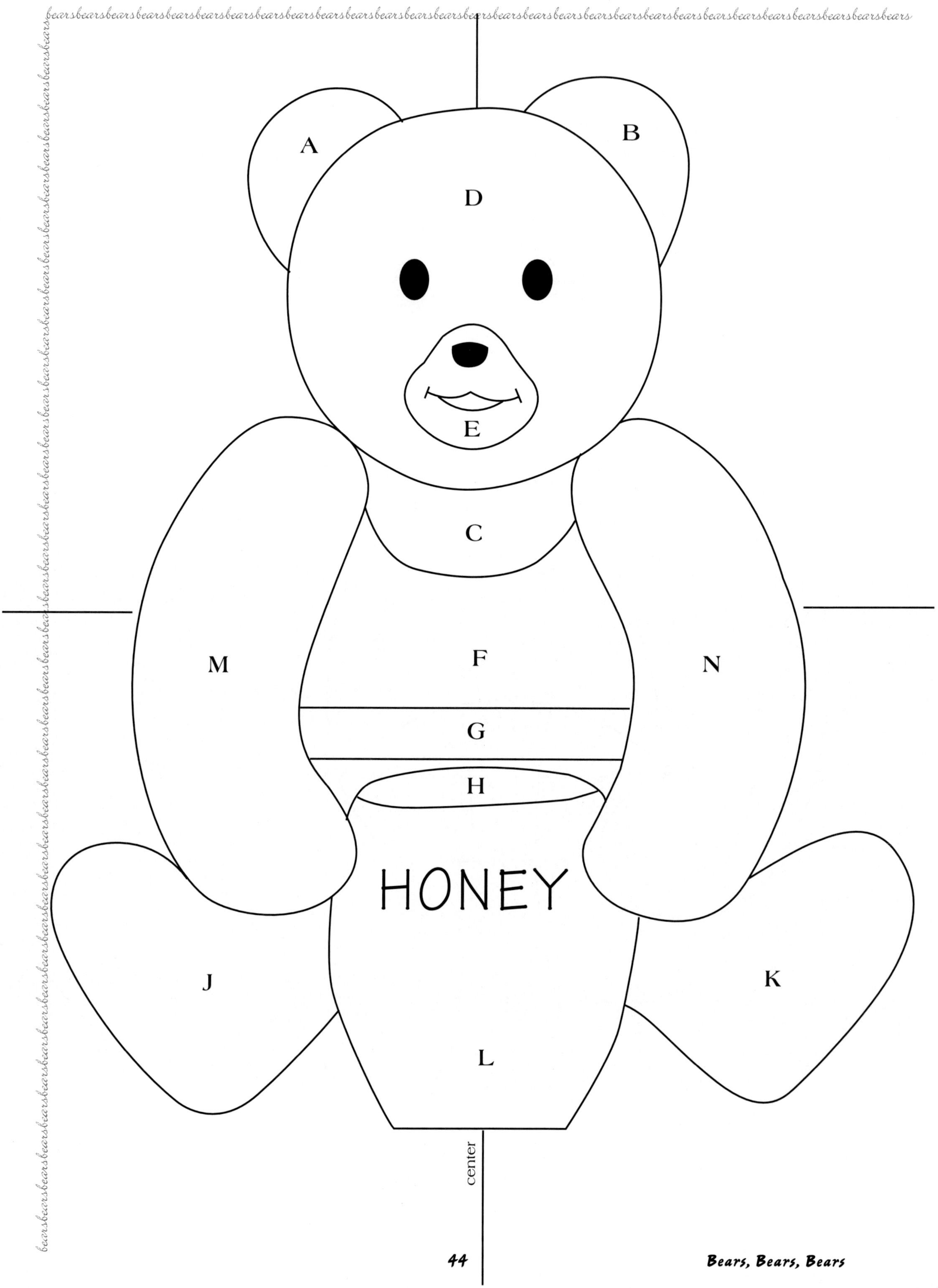

A

B

D

E

C

M

F

N

G

H

HONEY

J

K

L

center

bias

Appliqué bias
strip first

A

B

L

N

O

O

C

E

D

L

M

K

J

Keep sides of K & J open
where L & M meet

H

F

G

Center

F

D

E

A

G

B

C

H

J

K

L

M

Center

46

Bears, Bears, Bears

Center

N

M

O

A

B

K

L

E

C

D

J

H

F

G